Pulchritudinous Poetry

THE BODY EARTH

VOLUME I OF THE SERIES

A Journey of Self Through the Elements

Michelle Bravo

Pulchritudinous Poetry

The Body Earth

Volume I of the Series,

A Journey of Self Through the Elements

Copyright © July 2012, Michelle Bravo

ISBN-10: 0615544193

EAN-13: 9780615544199

ALL RIGHTS RESERVED. This book contains material protected under International and Federal Copyright Laws and Treaties. Any unauthorized reprint or use of this material is prohibited. No part of this book may be reproduced or transmitted in any form or by any means, electronic or mechanical, including photocopying, recording, or by any information storage and retrieval system without express written permission from the author / publisher.

*For Ray of Light, thank you
for persevering with me through it all...*

Pulchritudinous Poetry
THE BODY EARTH

Preface	vii
Catch and Release	3
Mercury Poisoning	7
Trust	11
From Orpheus to Eurydice	15
Is Your Heart Like An Orange?	19
Ties that Bind	23
Love Leash	27
I Held Myself Away Dare	31
Rough Sleeper	39
Persephone	43
A Woman's Impertinence	47
My Beloved	53
Dolor	57

Human Experience on Earth and the Physical Body

Pulchritudinous Poetry – THE BODY EARTH is the first in a series of five volumes. Each volume is based on one of the five elements of the Godai. The Godai is described in Japanese philosophy as:

Earth (*Chi*) – Physical Body, Stability, Gravity

Water (*Sui*) – Emotion, Intuition, Adaptability

Wind (*Fū*) – Intellect, Communication, Wisdom

Fire (*Ka*) – Drive, Motivation, Passion

Aether (*Kū*) – Upper Sky, Space, Void

Being human is a whole, elementally-based experience that begins and ends with the body. Lessons learned in daily life while living on earth are only possible and understood thanks to the physical body.

The body hears, smells, feels, tastes and touches through life. The body is without apology, shame or questioning in its needs, wants and desires. In its pure, simple, animal form, the body is perfectly childlike in its demands. There is integrity in the body in that, unlike the mind and emotions, it never lies.

Pulchritudinous Poetry – THE BODY EARTH was brought into being thanks to an inspirational poetry reading I attended via the Bohemian Socials group in San Francisco, CA. The poems that continued to flow from me thanks to that initial reading were further inspired by a relationship that began late 2010. I have included body-inspired poems written in previous years to round out the volume.

For me, poetry can be as precious as a satin box of very rich chocolate. Each one savored and experienced for its individual affect on the senses.

May the poetry herein afford you at least one delicious, savory moment of recognition and thankfulness in the exquisiteness of your own body.

Michelle Bravo

October 17, 2011

Catch and Release

6/19/11

Diving and swooning
swirling and hurling
tempting, delectable
Bait
The smallest of samplings
Just barely a nudge
and I'm hooked
As You patiently
Wait
A stinging, sharp bite
A swish and a flash
And suddenly, gasping for
Air
Put me back! Put me back!
Back where?
Back down there!
Back deep in the
warmth of my
Lair

The smell of You
sticks to my sides
Your fingerprint
marked my left eye

Catch and release me
And next time I'll err
on caution's side of the port
For there's nothing worse
to be lured
from the depths
to the surface
Caught only for sport

Mercury poisoning

3/19/11

Elegantly packaged

gift wrapped

In deep purples, burgundy and black

Once opened

Untouchable

as silver Mercury

Enticing

Slippery

Deadly

Life-threateningly hypnotized

by your lithe soft-firmness

beckoning me to my

Eventual demise…

(And my mother called ME Medusa!?!)

Your soft, dark ribbons
Lace themselves through my hair
They brush gently across my pale cheek
slipping 'round my throat
occluding my breath
retarding my speech

My brain
Cumbrous
thickened with despair

My movement
Asphyxiated
Dazed, clumsy

My words
when freed
come chortling
out of me in
a nonsensical jumble
Steadily
Unhurriedly
I am readily poisoned by you

Trust

5/28/11

Trust is a thing with plucked feathers
Long after the beauty's bygone
still provides warmth and solace
though prickly, worn and foregone

Trust is a pair of silk slippers
Worn 'til both soles are thin
tho' dirty, torn and ragged
O'er time, softer, without and within

Trust is a love that keeps challenging
to push me and prod me to grow
bristly, sometimes and demanding
My biggest leaps in trust are those
keeping me present and here
Not back in the past over there

Nostalgia's the algae
that clouds me
choking my liquid resolve
abducting my reason it binds me
While Trust keeps me here and in love

From Orpheus to Eurydice

03/19/11

I am gilded and gold
All scarlet readiness
and blithe darkness
Surging far ahead of you

My words
Musical
Siren-like
Deep
Opaque
they drown
your memories
of others before me

Like Orpheus
for his beloved
Eurydice

I longed to rescue
you from your unconscious
walking-dead state

You began
With patient steps
following me
into aliveness
once again

If only I did not
Look back
Impatiently, I looked back…

You have returned to your
Underworld
Surface
I to my
Surface
Underworld

Tell me…
When?
Where?
Will We At Last Meet?

Is your heart like an orange?

Written in 2002, for B.J.

Is your heart like an orange
Hard and cold from the fridge
To be held in my hands
'Til made warm?

Do the juices inside it
Taste of sweetness
while biting it
or sour
and filled with scorn?

Burgess remarked
free-will is blocked
by horrific conditioned
experience

In the meantime

I'll cry

I'll wheedle

I'll try

To continue my

worship and reverence

Ties that Bind

4/24/11

Loneliness, the sometime step-sister to Solitude,
is a sort of self-induced exile
into a corridor of great gray walls of pock-marked
cement with chunks torn out and ribs of rusted iron
protruding from them
ready to sharply bite
into my tender flesh
if I stop paying attention to where I'm going

Fear is the disgustingly obese,
traumatized mother of Loneliness
She has always favored Solitude
Yet despises the mere existence of Loneliness
Even though it was she who gave birth to her

Fear heavily crushes, pulverizes
grinds the breath from My Self
thickens My Self's blood with sugary
despair

My Self cries,
"Come! Come meet your new lover!"
"He'll lift you out of this."
Referring, of course, to that
White Knight of all Knights
Self-Sufficiency

Love Leash

4/25/11

Love is a string
a golden cord that pulls
from the end of the tip
of my left ring finger
deep into the fathoms of my heart
It wraps itself several times 'round
binding me tightly to You

The sight of You
catches my breath
my captured heart
expands…but only so far

The faded smell of You
on my pillow
tingles my toes
loosens the cord

then quickly corrects
at the memory of You

Like a dog on a leash
I am pulled to and fro
Looking deep into Your eyes
for guidance
for absolution
for asking
for a modicum
of the freedom
I had before You

Will you be Kind
Or Cruel,
as my heart's
New Master?

I held myself away

3/27/11

I held myself away from you
Marking every day
with dash marks, hash marks
Blithe remarks
Physically an adult
Emotionally a girl

With patience, fortitude and joy
You allowed me
time to dance

To whirl and twirl
Spin out of control
'Til at last I could take no more

And as I fell clumsily
to the floor
After dancing with another

You offered up
Your pale hand
And touched my cheek
As you scooped me up

You lifted me up
And brushed me off
Holding me close
As you had all along

My Mother
My Father
My Husband
My One

Dare

7/18/11

I dare you to scare me
Unfreeze me
And Cure me
from these torrid nightmares
Uplift me
Unbind me
from this place of blank stares
I dare you

I dare you to ride me
to bone me
inspire me
to leave all the rest
Cum at my behest
I dare you

I dare you to hold me
to spoon me
and fight me
to take up my glove
Be challenged in love
And never, ever release me
I dare you

Rough Sleeper

Written, 2007 for J.B.

It's cold
Like nobody's business cold
Like sheets of icy rain
Along the coast with
Wind that cuts across
My face

The metal shell
The vehicle
Does little to keep it out

Needles and Insulin
Sharpness and Life
How is it these two go together?
I wish I knew

The needle is cold
It cuts my skin
While insulin burns

And chills me

It's worse than
Outside cold
because
It's with me
Inside
Every day

Jesus shed blood
For our sins
And Died

I shed blood
every day
And Live
In spite of my sins

Persephone

3/19/11

Eyes averted, yes…
For fear of being whisked away
Abducted eternally

A modern-day Persephone
Hypnotized
Seduced
Led to a venerable feast in an underworld of
the senses never to return fully to Light

Completely held by the whims of
One who knows my body's secrets
And reveals them all to me

Each touch, each kiss, each deep penetration
The equivalent of a dark, jeweled seed
Plucked from a carefully ensconced, tightly

Held roundness that even when removed
Leaves a perfect impression of what was

Once felt and consumed, further entrances
And leaves a particular emptiness that cannot
And will not be duplicated by anyone else again

Languid yet deeply enthralled, my eyes
Stay averted to ensure i may yet escape
Your silky tendrils of psychic cords i've allowed
To enwrap me in my dreams, in my thoughts
And my life

This above all from You,
My beautiful, sensuous, electrifying arachnid
You have effectively stunned me

Like a tightly bound, feathery moth
Caught in a stickily frustrating web,
i am slowly losing
my desire to escape
as i realize it's simply
too late for me to do so

A Woman's Impertinence

06/26/11

Vexed and perplexed
I sit here alone
As I ponder my piteous state

I broke My own rules with You
This part I know so why do I choose
to still wait?

No reason or rhyme
Explains how this time
My loathing ran wild
like a beast

Aversion, repulsion
It's always the same
As I can't comprehend
in the least

Why you place them before Me
Before Yourself too
Frustrating
Enraging
Absurd!

Crack the whip on the cow
That one you're with now
Who's a slow and contemptible
Turd

You asked me to love them
As if they're my own?
Haha! Well, that's quite a stretch

Vying for Time
Theirs against Mine
Why should I?
They're not of MY flesh

Supposedly ruled
By biology's clock
For Me?
What a boatload, a crock!

I'll not harm
My body

My vessel
My temple
nor place it in danger or shock

Producing and breeding
Like that cow with her calves?
Honey, I'm not Your beloved livestock

I enjoy Our connection
the sex
the affection
and love to make love in that way

But to bear the end product
of all of these things?
Ha!
You've got to be kidding me!?!

Maybe I'm vicious, cruel and possessed
as judged by society's creed
My impertinence stands
just as sure as my hands
are typing this rant, this decree

I'm Female
You know this
I'm selfish as well
with passion
to the nth degree

If you can't take a stand
for Yourself, My good man
for now love, I surely must flee

My Beloved

01/10/11

My beloved is richly
scented
A sweetness
that tonifies every
Part of me
My purest most
submissive trust
I give to only Him

He is quick
Smooth, supple
His lips light as
a moth's tongue
against my skin

We move together as
beautifully

coiled snakes
Equally cunning,
Hypnotic
Loving

His actions methodic
achingly slow
yet foundational
as they speak firmly of
and to his intentions
with me

He is both darkness and light
Secretive yet vastly open
I feel him through
to his very depths
Thus, distance
has no meaning
for us

When I embrace Him
All of Him
I am not separate
Only further enhanced
In our togetherness

We inspire each other
through liveliest of
conversations
where Time & Space
are meaningless

We are One
yet parallel
within our oneness

Reveling in each other
as unique, glittering
bits of sand against
the vast expanse
of a universal sea
of perseverance, wealth
and consciousness